Things That Sting

Sea Anemones

By Walter LaPlante

Gareth Stevens
PUBLISHING

Please visit our website, www.garethstevens.com. For a free color catalog of all our high-quality books, call toll free 1-800-542-2595 or fax 1-877-542-2596.

Library of Congress Cataloging-in-Publication Data

LaPlante, Walter.
Sea anemones / by Walter LaPlante.
p. cm. — (Things that sting)
Includes index.
ISBN 978-1-4824-1711-1 (pbk.)
ISBN 978-1-4824-1712-8 (6-pack)
ISBN 978-1-4824-1710-4 (library binding)
1. Sea anemones — Juvenile literature. I. Title.
QL377.C7 L37 2015
593.6—d23

First Edition

Published in 2016 by
Gareth Stevens Publishing
111 East 14th Street, Suite 349
New York, NY 10003

Designer: Nicholas Domiano
Editor: Kristen Rajczak

Photo credits: Cover, p. 1 Sergio Bertino/Shutterstock.com; title texture: Asya Alexandrova/ Shutterstock.com; caption box: VectorShots/Shutterstock.com; p. 5 Aleksey Stemmer/ Shutterstock.com; p. 7 Sharon Eisenzopf/Shutterstock.com; p. 9 (both) NatureDiver/ Shutterstock.com; p. 11 Rostislav Ageev/Shutterstock.com; p. 13 Stephen P Parker/ Photo Researchers/Getty Images; p. 15 De Agostini Picture Library/Getty Images; p. 17 Dan Herrick/Lonely Planet Images/Getty Images; p. 19 Joze Maucec/Shutterstock.com; p. 20 Bart Braun/Wikimedia Commons.

Printed in the United States of America

CPSIA compliance information: Batch #CS15GS: For further information contact Gareth Stevens, New York, New York at 1-800-542-2595.

Contents

Words in the glossary appear in **bold** type the first time they are used in the text.

Sea Flowers

Have you ever seen a sea anemone (uh-NEH-muh-nee)? It's a **marine** animal that looks somewhat like a flower! In fact, sea anemones are named for a flower called the anemone.

Sea anemones are invertebrates, which means they have no backbone. They're part of the animal group *Cnidaria* (ny-DEHR-ee-uh) that also includes coral and jellyfish. One feature that makes *Cnidarians* alike is their ability to sting! For a sea anemone, stinging is a way to protect and feed itself.

THAT SMARTS!

Sea anemones are half animal and half plant! Scientists still group them with animals, but have learned some of their body systems are closer to those of plants.

The largest sea anemones are the largest *Cnidarians*.

Living All Over

There are more than 1,000 species, or kinds, of sea anemones. Some are only 0.5 inch (1.27 cm) wide, while others are nearly 5 feet (1.5 m) in width!

Sea anemones are found in oceans around the world. Many live in the water near the shore and may even be uncovered when the tide is low. Sea anemones have been found to live deeper than 33,000 feet (10,000 m) below the ocean's surface, too. In 2013, scientists found sea anemones living under an ice sheet in Antarctica!

That Smarts!

Sea anemones can be most colors, including green, blue, and yellow. When seen in a group, they might look like a colorful flower garden!

The most—and most colorful—sea anemones are found in **tropical** waters.

Every Body

A sea anemone has a body shaped like a tube. It's hollow. At one end, it has a strong "foot" called a pedal disc. Sea anemones often use this foot to hold on to rocks and other hard surfaces or sand. It's sticky, too, so they can stay in place easily.

At the other end of the tube-shaped body is a mouth. Surrounding the mouth are **tentacles** that look a bit like the petals on a flower.

THAT SMARTS!

A sea anemone's body can be long and thin or short and thick.

Even though sea anemones can be different sizes and colors, they all have a similar body, like the one shown here.

Terrible Tentacles

Sea anemones' tentacles often look pretty, waving slowly in the ocean. But they're dangerous! The tentacles are covered with thousands of special **cells** called nematocysts (nih-MAA-tuh-sihsts). Each nematocyst contains a tiny coiled thread that's **barbed** and full of **venom**.

The tentacles are very **sensitive**. The nematocysts will "fire" their venomous threads at the slightest touch. While each thread only has a small amount of venom in it, many are fired at once. This can be very painful for the animal that's getting fired at!

THAT SMARTS!

Other animals, such as jellyfish, have nematocysts, too.

Sea anemone tentacles commonly occur in multiples of six.

Silent Predators

Because of their stinging tentacles, sea anemones are deadly predators. They often stay in one place and wait for food to come to them. And they'll eat just about anything that does! This includes fish, shrimp, crabs, and other marine animals.

Once prey touches a sea anemone's tentacles and the nematocysts fire their venomous threads, the prey may be killed. Or the venom **paralyzes** them. The sea anemone then uses its tentacles to move the prey to its mouth.

THAT SMARTS!

*Sea anemones can **digest** prey in about 15 minutes!*

Sea anemones swallow their prey whole! They "spit out" parts they can't digest, such as shells and bones.

Some Protection

Sea anemones' stinging tentacles help protect them from predators, too. Most animals don't want to chow down on something sharp and venomous! But some animals, such as sea slugs, aren't harmed by sea anemones' venom. They'll eat sea anemones, tentacles and all. Butterfly fish will rip off a sea anemone's tentacles and then eat the rest.

To escape a predator, sea anemones can unstick their foot and float or swim away by twisting their body. They can also pull their tentacles in.

THAT SMARTS!

Sea stars, eels, codfish, and flounder are other sea anemone predators.

These moray eels are hiding among the sea anemones.
Could they want a snack?

Not Clowning Around

Some sea anemones have an unlikely protector: the clown fish. The clown fish chases predator fish away from its home in the anemone. It also cleans the anemone! In turn, the clown fish can eat the scraps of the sea anemone's food.

Scientists don't know for sure why clown fish living in sea anemones aren't stung. One idea is that the clown fish touch a few of the anemone's tentacles each day starting when they're babies. They then form protective **mucus** that keeps them safe—but only in their home anemone.

That Smarts!

The clown fish is protected from predators among the tentacles of the sea anemone. The anemone can then eat the predators trying to eat the clown fish!

The clown fish and sea anemone are an example of symbiosis, or the cooperation of two unlike animals living together for the benefit of both.

Stinging Each Other?

Though slow moving—or often unmoving—some kinds of sea anemones battle each other to guard their territory. They live in big groups near other groups of anemones. There's space between them that shouldn't be crossed.

Around the edges of these groups are anemones with tentacles that have even stronger stinging abilities. These "warriors" sting any anemones from another group that come too close. The **intruding** anemone might sting back—and one or both may die from the battle.

THAT SMARTS!

Sometimes, a sea anemone reproduces by splitting in half! It can also break off a part of its body to grow into another adult anemone.

Sea anemones need to be in the water most of the time. Those that live on rocks in shallow waters can dry out and die if the tide is out for too long.

Take Care

Most sea anemones can't hurt people. But sea anemones in one group are known as stinging anemones because they can sting humans and harm them. They look more like coral than other sea anemones and are found in the Indo-Pacific Ocean. The Bali fire anemone is one of these.

Be careful no matter where you come across a sea anemone. This is for your own safety, as well as the well-being of this fascinating marine animal!

Watch out! This stinging anemone could hurt you.

Sea Anemone Facts

size	0.5 inch (1.27 cm) to 5 feet (1.5 m) wide
color	all colors
species	more than 1,000
life span	can live 60–80 years; some live even longer
range	oceans all over the world; found on shallow, rocky shores and deeper than 33,000 feet (10,000 m)
prey	fish, crabs, shrimp
predators	sea slugs, butterfly fish, eels

Glossary

barbed: having a barb, or a sharp point that bends backwards and isn't easy to remove

cell: the smallest basic part of a living thing

digest: to break down food inside the body so that the body can use it

intruding: entering without invitation

marine: having to do with the sea

mucus: a thick slime produced by the bodies of many animals

paralyze: to make unable to move

sensitive: able to easily sense or feel changes in surroundings

tentacle: a long, thin body part that sticks out from an animal's head or mouth

tropical: having to do with the warm parts of Earth near the equator

venom: something an animal makes in its body that can harm other animals

For More Information

Books

Didier, Dominique A. *Strange Sea Creatures: Sea Anemone*. Ann Arbor, MI: Cherry Lake Publishing, 2015.

Schueller, Gretel H. *Cnidarians: Jellyfish, Corals, Sea Anemones, and Their Relatives*. New York, NY: Chelsea House, 2012.

Websites

Photo Gallery: Sea Anemones
ocean.nationalgeographic.com/ocean/photos/sea-anemone/
Check out lots of pictures of sea anemones from National Geographic.

Ranger Rick: Sea Anemones
nwf.org/Kids/Ranger-Rick/Animals/Fish/Sea-Anemones.aspx
Learn more about sea anemones and other animals on this website just for kids.

Index